SPEECH

OF

HON. FRANCIS W. KELLOGG,

OF MICHIGAN,

IN THE HOUSE OF REPRESENTATIVES, JUNE 12, 1860.

The House being in Committee of the Whole on the state of the Union—

Mr. KELLOGG said:

Mr. CHAIRMAN: Since I took my seat as a member of the Thirty-sixth Congress, I have not consumed the time of the House in debate, but listened with patience, and often with profit, to the eloquent gentlemen on both sides who have led in these discussions, and contented myself with voting as I thought the interests of my constituents and the country demanded. But this session will soon close, and I wish to express my opinion of the political questions before the House and the country, and respectfully ask the attention of gentlemen for the brief period of time allowed me.

The people of the United States will soon be called on to select a Chief Magistrate for the Republic, and determine, according to the forms of law, the political character of the next Congress that shall assemble here. Already the note of preparation is sounding throughout the country, and the principles of the different parties are everywhere discussed. The representatives of the Republican party recently assembled at Chicago, and declared their belief in the necessity of a return to those principles which prevailed in the administration of our national affairs for more than half a century. They also nominated an able and popular man for the Presidency, and I believe a large majority of the people will support him, and endeavor, by his election, to secure that change of policy and principles which we believe is so necessary to the prosperity of the nation.

The revenue laws need remodeling immediately. The present tariff operates injuriously to the interests of the whole country, while at the same time it does not produce sufficient revenue for the wants of the government. All parties agree in taxing imports for the support of government, and I do not think that policy will ever be departed from. The only question is in reference to the manner in which those duties shall be imposed. The Democratic party propose to raise the necessary revenue, without inquiring as to the effect of the course pursued upon the business of the country. Government, in their estimation, has nothing to do with that. It may be constitutional and eminently proper for the government to employ all its power in protecting the slave property of a few Southern gentlemen who may emigrate to our Territories, but protection to FREE LABOR is a very different thing; and grave doubts are expressed at once as to the right of the government to meddle at all in such a matter.

The Republican party believe it to be the DUTY of the national government to promote the GENERAL WELFARE, by affording adequate protection to the industrial interests of the American people, against all foreign competition whatsoever. They do not ask protection for one class or one section of the country at the expense of another, but demand the adoption of a wise policy, which shall benefit the business of the whole country. This, we believe, can be accomplished in the imposition of duties, by a proper discrimination in favor of those interests which need the foster-

---

Polkinhorn's Steam Printing Office, D street, bet. 6th & 7th sts

ing aid of government. Why *any one* should object to this policy I cannot understand. All history is fruitful of facts in its favor. Never, in any country, have manufactories been established in the face of free trade with other nations, and without that protection government only can bestow.

I like the teachings of the New Testament on questions of political economy. St. Paul bids us "Do good unto *all* men as we have opportunity, BUT ESPECIALLY TO THE HOUSEHOLD OF FAITH." That is, take care of yourselves and your own families and country first, and then do good unto others as opportunity offers.

Self-preservation or protection is the first law of nature, and as necessary to nations as individuals. Our true policy is to import no more than our natural exports will pay for, and thus keep the most of the gold we have in our own country, instead of sending it to Europe. In this way we shall build up manufactories of our own, and furnish constant and profitable employment for our laboring men. The farmer would have a good home market, with steady prices, for his produce, and the whole country would prosper. Under this policy, England has become the wealthiest nation in the world, and if we are wise we shall follow her example.

I appeal to the WORKINGMEN of the land for their support, for it is of more importance to the labor than the capital of the country. Let the policy of the Democratic party be persevered in a few years longer, and our workingmen would be reduced to the condition of slaves, deprived of the luxuries of life and toiling for a bare subsistence. But adopt the policy we advocate, and enforce it permanently, and the result will be GOOD WAGES for the workingmen, GOOD PRICES for the products of our farmers, and a GOLD CURRENCY for the business of the country. Its beneficent influences would extend to every part of the nation, and our whole country would rapidly become rich, powerful, and independent.

Our policy in relation to the public lands is well understood by the people, and meets with their unqualified approval. The homestead bill, as it passed this House, must, sooner or later, become a law, and under its operation our national domain, no longer monopolized by speculators, will be converted into homes for an intelligent and hardy yeomanry—the fit custodians of the liberties of their country.

The Republican party are in favor of making such appropriations for light-houses, harbors, and other facilities to navigation, as are necessary to the prosperity of the growing commerce on the great lakes of the Northwest. The past and present Democratic administrations have paid no attention to our wants, and I feel assured that we need not hope for any until the Republican party are in power. I am no advocate of any extended system of internal improvements, for the benefit of particular localities only; but this commerce of the lakes is national in its character, and can no more be called *local* than that of the Atlantic.

If it is the duty of the national government to construct harbors on the seaboard, it is just as clearly their duty to construct them along the thousands of miles of our lake coasts, so that our commercial marine may find a refuge in rough weather, and life and property be safe from the fury of the elements. The average loss on these lakes is twice as great, in proportion to the number of men and vessels employed, as it is on the Atlantic.

I have no recent account of the annual losses on these lakes, but learn, from an official document before me, that in four years previous to and ending in 1851, over FIVE HUNDRED LIVES were lost, and upwards of TWO MILLIONS of dollars worth of property. This loss falls almost exclusively on the early settlers of a new country, and is owing mainly to the absence of harbors, and obstructions to the entrance of those which do exist. Surely something should be done by the national government to save these men, who are subduing the wilderness and who traffic on these waters, from so much suffering and loss.

Sir, these lakes would be called SEAS in the old world. They cover over ninety thousand square miles, and constitute a great national and continental highway for the trade of the United States and British America. On one side they are the boundary of several large and powerful States, and on the other of a portion of the British empire. A large number of vessels now leave the lake ports for Europe, and a great and rapidly increasing commerce is carried on upon them between the different States and British America.

Buffalo, Cleveland, Detroit, Milwaukie, and Chicago are the principal cities; and, though nothing but villages thirty years ago, the tonnage of either one of them now exceeds that of any Southern city, except New Orleans. The tonnage of Chicago is seven thousand tons larger than that of Charleston. Her receipts of lumber exceed those of any other port in the country, and her exports of grain are larger than those of any city in the world. To accommodate this vast trade, great numbers of vessels arrive and depart daily, and a forest of masts may be seen extending for miles up the river. And yet, sir, it is not unusual to see vessels aground at the mouth of her harbor. To enter it is difficult always, and in a gale almost impossible; though a small sum judiciously expended would make it accessible at all times, and perfectly secure. Through the vigilance of her Representative here, a small appropriation for this purpose was smuggled into a bill at the last session, which the President was obliged to sign; but even that was not applied as it should have been. Those who delude themselves and others with the idea that the Democracy will ever do anything for our harbors, should have been in this House a few weeks ago, when an attempt was made to pass a resolution directing the Secretary of War to expend the balance of this appropriation at once for the improvement of that harbor. Why, sir, twenty members sprang to their feet at once in opposition. One might have thought they had been suddenly seized with St. Vitus' dance, and *could'nt* sit still when such a measure was before us.

Illinois and Michigan have each of them furnished Demcratic leaders of distinction, and immense majorities at one time, to support them in all their measures, but what have they done for the commerce of the lakes? Nothing at all. In their anxiety to get into the White House, they have forgotten their constituents, and neglected their interests entirely. Perhaps I had better say that they are opposed to appropriations for these purposes. "Tax the tonnage that enters your port," says one of them, "and build your own harbors. It is not the duty of the government to construct works of this character!" Yet this Democratic leader thinks we had better buy Cuba, at a cost of *three hundred millions* of dollars, and thus get a few more Senators who would always be ready to take Western interests by the throat when opportunity offered. *That* is constitutional, as everything is that has a look southward, and tends to the advancement of Southern interests. But the men who fell the forests of Michigan, or till the praries of Illinois, must take care of themselves; and if, in getting their lumber and grain to market, a few hundred men and a few millions of dollars are lost annually, on national waters, for want of good harbors, what does this government care for that? They have nothing to do with it; but let a Southern planter call on the President or his officers to catch a fugitive slave, or punish some man who dared to give one a supper and bid him God-speed, and troops, telegraphs, and railroads are put in motion if needed, and money cheerfully expended to any amount, no matter what it may cost; and no one must presume to question the constitutionality of it. The reason is perfectly plain, and easily comprehended. The interests of the farmers and lumbermen of the West are *local* and *sectional* in their nature, but catching fugitive slaves is a *national* affair, and must be attended to by the government.

There is one great natural obstruction to lake navigation, known as the St. Clair Flats, and near the borders of the State of Michigan, of which I wish to speak particularly. The water here for a short distance is at times very shallow, and ordinary vessels frequently get aground there and suffer seriously from delay and expense in getting off. A small sum of money, properly laid out, would deepen the channel so vessels could pass over them without difficulty or delay.

Few persons have any conception of the magnitude of the commerce that asks for this relief at the hands of the general government. Captain Graham, of the topographical corps of engineers, informs us that in 1855 the value of all the articles of commerce and navigation passing over the St. Clair Flats exceeded *two hundred and fifty-nine millions of dollars!* He estimates the increase on the rates of freights in consequence of these obstructions at more than two million dollars per annum—one-half of which falls on the farmers of the West, being so much taken from the value of their produce. Congress, at the last session, made an appropriation to complete this improvement, but the President vetoed the bill. His reason was the unconstitutionality of such appropriations. In his opinion, government has nothing to do with it, and he says further, "When the State of Michigan shall cease to depend on the Treasury of the United States, I doubt not that she, in conjunction with Upper Canada, will provide the necessary means for keeping this work in repair, in the least expensive and effective manner, and without being burdensome to any interest."

Mr. Chairman, I know of no reason why Michigan should be taunted with being dependent on the Treasury of the United States. Is it because the Northwestern States, of which Michigan is but one, demand the improvement of the navigation of these national waters by the general government? I believe these States contribute their share of the money in our national treasury, which is ever open to receive what we give, but never to disburse for our benefit. The President would have Michigan enter into an alliance with Canada, and make this improvement, and then tax the tonnage passing until they are paid. But the Constitution prohibits the State of Michigan from entering into any treaty or alliance, for this or any other purpose, with Canada, or any other country. I know Congress may consent to let Michigan enter into such an arrangement with Canada, but this is a policy we should never encourage. Let the national government transact all our business with foreign powers. This is my first objection to the course recommended by the President.

In the next place, the compact between the States and the Northwest Territory, entered into before the formation of our Constitution, and whose validity and perpetual obligation is asserted and secured by the 6th article of that instrument, declares that these waters "SHALL BE COMMON PROPERTY, (or highways,) AND FOREVER FREE, as well to the inhabitants of the said country as to the citizens of the United States and those of any other State admitted into the confederacy, WITHOUT ANY TAX, DUTY, OR IMPOST THEREFOR."

In my judgment, this settles the question, and the national government must remove these obstacles to navigation, or they must remain forever. If there was a decent pretext on the part of the government for this parsimony and meanness toward the West, I could endure it better. But there is none—none whatever. Look at the manner in which money is expended in other sections of the country. A liberal appropriation was made a few years ago to build new custom-houses at Charleston and New Orleans. By a gross abuse of power on the part of our executive officers, plans were adopted for their construction involving a much larger outlay than was contemplated by Congress, and year after year we have been called on for more. Well, sir, some four millions have been expended on the two buildings already, and I believe it is estimated that at least two millions more will be necessary to their completion.

Sir, I am willing to erect expensive and costly buildings in such cities, but I submit that one million dollars is enough to build a custom-house in *either* of those cities—enough to rear a magnificent structure of marble, large enough for all the business that would need to be transacted in them till they should crumble into dust.

Suppose they had taken the two millions for the two custom-houses, and given us the remaining four millions to build our harbors and improve the navigation of the lakes. It would have given an immense impulse to our trade, saved many valuable lives and millions of dollars worth of property. But we need not speculate on suppositions like these, for no appropriations will be made for the benefit of Western commerce till the reign of the Democratic party is ended. That day, if I read the signs of the times aright, is not far distant. The people of the West are sick of this sectional and extravagant appropriation of the public money. Their commerce may suffer on national waters, for the want of a few thousand dollars to improve their navigation, while half a dozen millions are expended in erecting a couple of palatial custom-houses in the South.

The magnitude of the appropriations for such purposes compels attention. A million of dollars is an immense sum to expend on any public building. If it were all in silver coin, it would weigh over forty tons. Yes, sir, FORTY TONS, or well nigh A HUNDRED CART LOADS OF SILVER DOLLARS — to *build* a couple of custom-houses? No, sir, to *begin* them. It will take *six times* that sum, or TWO HUNDRED AND FORTY TONS OF SILVER DOLLARS, to complete them.

If we continue building custom-houses after this fashion, it will take all the gold in California ere we have supplied the whole Republic. But of this there is probably no danger. Such heavy showers of gold fall only in Southern latitudes. Not a drop of it reaches that part of the Republic I have the honor to represent.

The cause of this is found in the fact that Southern politicians control the Democratic party now, as they always have done from the first hour of its existence. They profess to believe the interests of the South are injured by a protective policy—though to be sure they all unite in demanding a good duty on sugar; but that is a

Southern product, and of course it is constitutional to protect it. They misrepresent the friends of protection also, by affirming that they wish to tax the industry of one section of the country for the benefit of another. This is not so. All parties agree in raising the revenue for the support of the government by a tax on imports; and WE say, that in imposing these duties it is better for the *whole* country, North and South, to *discriminate in favor of American industry.* They do not believe government has anything to do in this matter, however, but their practice is and has been to discriminate *against* American industry, to the great injury of FREE LABOR, and we believe to the injury of the whole country. They are opposed, also, to expending any money for constructing harbors and benefitting commerce, except upon the seaboard, where nearly *all their interests* are.

A few years ago the South was divided upon these questions, but the politicians of the Democratic party conceived the idea of uniting the whole South in support of what they termed its true policy, and cast about for means to effect it. There was but one way, and that was, to bring the question of slavery into politics. By playing on this "harp of a thousand strings," they hoped to create a great sectional party, who, under Southern leaders, would be able to keep possession of the national government, with all its power and patronage, and control its whole policy forever.

Sir, the scheme worked well, and its success justified the sagacity of its originators. I know they have persistently affirmed that the North began this political agitation, but that statement was necessary to their success, and has been reiterated so often, that some who know better believe it now. They commenced by an assault upon the North, because a few persons petitioned Congress on the subject of slavery. A just regard for the rights of the people would have led them to receive their petitions with respect, and report upon them, refusing their prayer, if not right to grant it. But this was foreign to their purpose; an excitement must be got up North and South; so the petitioners were kicked out of Congress, and this time-honored privilege denied. Emboldened by their success, they now determined to assail liberty in its very citadel. They denied the right to free speech, and demanded the suppression of anti-slavery papers by law. They called upon their friends at the North to stop all discussion of the question of slavery, by law if possible, if not by force. They found willing tools everywhere, and meetings were broken up by mobs, and one of them ended in the murder of Lovejoy, of Illinois. This created a great excitement and profound feeling among good men everywhere. They regarded a free press as the palladium of the people's liberties, and resented this unjustifiable assault upon the rights of freemen. The people of the Southern States may, if they choose, prevent the publication of anything in their jurisdiction against human bondage; but the Northern press will remain *forever free* to print what they please about the institutions of any country; and if slavery can't stand this free discussion, *so much the worse for slavery.* We can't help it; we ask for no political action against slavery in the States.

The general government has no right to meddle with it, then, directly or indirectly, and nobody desires it to do so. No, sir; slavery may exist in the Southern States as long as it can maintain itself against the public sentiment of the civilized world. If right in itself, it will continue as long as society and government exists; if wrong, it must gradually go down, and no power can preserve it from extinction. The agitation of this question in Congress, and the constant discussion of it, to the great detriment of the public business, is a curse to the whole country, and deeply to be deplored. But the Democratic party began it, and are responsible to the country for its continuance.

There is no good reason for it whatever. Southern men know perfectly well that neither slavery or the rights of slaveholders are in danger from any action of the general government. The honorable gentleman from Virginia (Mr. MILLSON) admitted this in a recent speech on this floor. Said he, "Sir, I say for one, *I do not fear the Republican party in any of its assaults upon slavery. I am not sensitive, because I do not fear you, gentlemen. You can do nothing that I dread. You will do nothing that can alarm me. You maintain your organization, hoping that the strong anti-slavery sentiment which you attempt to nourish and perpetuate will induce the people to remain with you bound together as a Republican party; and when you are lifted into power, then you will give that protection to northern manufacturing and mining interests, and prosecute those grand and gaudy schemes of internal improvement, that you have been prevented for so many years from accomplishing by the stern opposition of the Democratic party.*"

Here, then, you see the real cause of all this excitement and agitation, and the continued discussion of the question in Congress. Sir, it is *not* because their institutions are in danger, but they desire to keep the South united on the Democratic platform, and secure the aid of enough of the timid, time-serving, office-seeking portion of the people of the North to enable them to keep possession of the government, with all its offices, honors, and influence.

When this Congress assembled, on the first Monday of December last, I *knew* the Republican party did not intend to introduce the question of slavery, and I anticipated very little excitement, except what might grow out of the proposed inquiry into the corruption of the present administration, and the unlawful means made use of for years past to carry its various measures and reward party favorites. But I was mistaken. The leaders of the Democratic party beheld the results of the late election with fear and trembling. Old Pennsylvania, who had decided so many a contest in their favor, was faithful to their bidding no longer. Even old Berks rose up in her majesty, and rebuked the traitors who had proved false to the people's interests. One district after another, in different sections of the country, deserted the banner of the party, and the indignation of the people, expressed in thunder tones, was heard at last in the Capitol by the conclave of conspirators against the liberties of their country. Something must be done at once, and in this emergency the Helper book was a perfect God-send to the fanatical leaders, now driven to desperation by their recent defeats and the fear of Republican ascendency in the House of Representatives, and they resolved to use it in such a manner as to increase the general excitement, under cover of which they hoped to glide into power once more and govern the country four years longer. Accordingly the honorable gentleman from Missouri introduced his famous resolution declaring, in substance, that no man ought to be Speaker of this House who had recommended the circulation of that book; and this was made a pretext for preventing the organization of the House, and for the utterance of the most insolent and unjustifiable harangues ever listened to, in any deliberative body, since constitutional government had an existence. Democratic members vied with each other in their efforts to villify the actions and motives of the Republicans. We were denounced as traitors to our country, as false to our constitutional obligations, and as striving to excite their slaves to insurrection, to wholesale murder, and servile war.

And what excuse was there for this? Some members of Congress, the candidate for Speaker among them, had signed a circular recommending the circulation of a compend of a book entitled "The Impending Crisis." It was a book written with some spirit and ability, by a Mr. Helper, of North Carolina, full of damaging facts against slavery, and addressed mainly to the non-slaveholders of his native State, and the South generally, advising them to commence an effort for the abolition of slavery. There was not a word in it addressed to the slaves, nor was he any more strong and violent in the language he used in addressing Southern freemen than Southern members of Congress are in the habit of using continually on the floor of this House. Books more intemperate in tone and language are published every year in any country where the press is free, and nobody is alarmed or troubled. The truth is, this was an assault on slavery not easily answered, and therefore it must be denounced day after day. It was assailed in the bitterest terms, and never shall I forget the amazement with which I heard the distinguished and honorable member from Virginia [Mr. MILLSON, page 21 Cong. Globe] say, that "One who consciously, deliberately, and of purpose, lent his name and influence to the propagation of such writings, is *not only not fit to be Speaker, but is not fit to live!*"

What a comment on the institutions of the South, and how incompatible must the existence of slavery be with that of liberty or liberal institutions!

The next text for abusive and treasonable speeches was the foray of John Brown, an old man who, with a score of followers, undertook to revolutionize Virginia, and set her slaves at liberty. The Republican party were denounced as the authors, aiders, and abetters of it, in language as violent and strong as men could coin for the occasion. The then governor of Virginia engaged heartily in the work of traducing tens of thousands of men who, in all good qualities, were the peers of any in the land. We were told, on his authority, that large bodies of men were gathering in different portions of the North for the purpose of invading Virginia and rescuing Brown from the gallows. The lightning flashed these falsehoods through the land for weeks together. The whole country was kept in a feverish and intense excitement. Military companies were called out in Virginia, and kept marching and countermarching,—and this action, and the high positions of the authors of these base libels upon Northern men, really made *some* honest men believe the statements were true. And yet there was NO foundation for *any* of them. No attempt to rescue Brown was ever made, or ever thought of. Where is that "carpet-bag full of letters," that was to criminate the leaders of the Republican party, and make them parties to this invasion of a sister State? Why is it, that this governor, who "*knows what rubies would not tempt him to reveal*" about the complicity of Northern men in this crime of John Brown, has never been summoned before the Senate Committee? The reason is plain: He had nothing to communicate! The whole story was trumped up with a hope that it might affect the organization of the House and the election of President. Sir, the crime of John Brown was a trifling one, compared with that of these men who labored to blacken and destroy the characters of thousands of good citizens where they had no opportunity to vindicate themselves, and defend their reputations.

But the chief actor in this scene has passed into an obscurity from which he can never emerge, and there I leave him.

Since the organization of the House weeks have been spent here and in the Senate in discussions in favor of the extension of slavery and its protection in the Territories of the United States. For this discussion I can see no good reason other than the one I have named: keeping the Democratic party bound together, and uniting the entire South.

Sir, it is true that Southern politicians say they must have more territory for the extension of slavery, and that if we prohibit this extension, we take the first step towards its abolition. So, then, I suppose we are to go on and conquer Mexico and Central America, and annex them at our leisure, that this Southern institution may have a chance to expand all it will. If this be so, sir, let us know it. I apprehend the people are not ready for carrying out this scheme of universal conquest, and that if they should conclude to annex more territory, they will be slow to consent to curse it with slavery.

But let us see how we stand now, and whether there is any necessity for the next twenty years for the acquisition of more territory, and the extension of slavery. Why, at this time the South has more than eight hundred and fifty thousand square miles of territory, or as much as Great Britain, Austria, France and Spain, and one hundred thousand square miles more than all the Northern States, including Kansas, and yet they *are suffering for the want of room to expand in.* They own the most of the valley of the Mississippi, the finest in the world; they have a beautiful climate and fertile soil generally, and long before this vast region can be well settled and tilled, it will contain a population twice as large as we now have in the United States.

Who does not see, then, that this talk about the necessity of expansion at present, is of a piece with all the rest, and a part of the scheme for uniting the South and continuing a great sectional party in power, who will administer the government on sectional principles, and for sectional purposes entirely—*that* section the SOUTH ALWAYS.

The Republican party are opposed to the extension of slavery, and since this discussion is forced upon us, I desire to express my convictions concerning this question, though in a very brief manner.

The American Revolution was not a contest for mere material advantage or political independence, but a struggle for the RIGHTS OF MAN. The Declaration of Independence was the platform of principles on which our fathers stood, and the inspiration of its doctrines created armies, and carried on the war that terminated in our independence. With a solemnity befitting the enunciation of principles that were to revolutionize the world, they declared that "We hold these truths to be self-evident: that all men are created equal; that they are endowed by their Creator with certain inalienable rights, among which are life, LIBERTY, and the pursuit of happiness." These, in their estimation, are the rights of *all* men, the birthright of every human being. It is fashionable now to ridicule this great charter of human rights, but the wisest men in Europe at that time read it with wonder and admiration. They looked upon Washington, Adams, Jefferson, Madison, and their illustrious associates, as Israel did upon Moses, when he came down from Mount Sinai, with the table of the ten commandments. No language seemed strong enough to speak their praises. They were, as patriots, models for all ages;

as statesmen, they exhibited in themselves a concentration of all the wisdom of the past; and as prophets they foresaw the future and knew how to frame institutions that would carry out their principles and make them universal. But these facts of history need no recital. These great men who founded our government and framed our constitution, found slavery in the country, and deplored its existence. Of this there is abundant proof. Washington declared his desire for its abolition, and affirmed that Virginia "must at a period not remote enact laws for the abolition of slavery." I might quote whole pages from his letters to the same purpose, but it is unnecessary. The language of Jefferson is equally well known, and his sentiments accorded with those of all the statesmen and patriots of the day.

Benjamin Franklin, the incarnation of the common sense of that day, and the first philosopher of the age he lived in, was also the first president of the first abolition society in the United States, in good old Pennsylvania, where he lived, and where he died. These men believed the doctrines of the Declaration of Independence, and believed also that they would be gradually reduced to practice, become the sentiment of the world, and work out the abolition of slavery at some period in the far off future. But the wise men of these days, who are the leaders of the Democratic party, have discovered that these men did not know much after all; some of them never had seen a cotton plantation, and did not know cotton would be king. They did not know how rapidly fortunes would be made in raising cotton and sugar by slave labor, and how easily people could live in Virginia by raising slaves, to sell when prices should come up, so a boy three years old would bring more money than a good span of horses.

Had they understood all this, they might have altered their minds, and concluded slavery was right. Under such circumstances, perhaps I had better not introduce their testimony, but I hope I shall be pardoned for repeating what Henry Clay said of extending slavery, as it is of a more recent date: "So long as God allows the vital current to flow through my veins, so long as reason holds her seat enthroned in my brain, I will never, never aid in submitting one rood of free territory to the everlasting curse of human bondage." I don't know that Democrats will consider him good authority, but he was looked upon as a great man by millions, who revere his memory; and I think he will be remembered and quoted, long after slavery is abolished and its defenders forgotten.

But let us examine this Territorial question. Southern politicians say the Territories are the common property of the people of all the States, and that the citizens of one section of the country have as good a right to remove to the Territories as those of another. This I admit, but the South claim the right to take their *slaves* and *slave laws* with them, and in this way virtually *exclude* Northern men altogether. This the South denies, and says the non-slaveholder can reside there as well as anywhere. Some of them can, for some love slavery as well as Southern men do, but the great body of Northern men do not, and cannot go into a slave Territory, without relinquishing the enjoyment of rights as dear as life itself. Let me suppose, another Kansas. Its fertile plains and prairies look invitingly to thousands, and soon you see a host of hardy men building their homes hard by some noble river, and laying the foundation for a fine city.

A few thousand settlers are soon scattered over the beautiful country, and among them many planters with their slaves. Laws, of course, must be enacted for their security, and let us mark their operation. I will not allude to all the ways they have to vex men brought up in a free State, but to some of them. A post office is established early, and the hardy pioneers are soon ready to take the papers published near their old homes, and read the news as they have always done. A club is formed, and twenty copies of the Tribune, and perhaps as many more of the Evening Post, are ordered. The bundle of papers comes to the office, and now the "irrepressible conflict" commences. In accordance with the decision of the Postmaster General, the postmaster refuses to deliver them. They are incendiary documents.

Their circulation puts the institution of slavery in peril, and must therefore be prohibited. Some of my constituents may be among these settlers, and learn, to their amazement, from the circular of the Postmaster General, that this petty minion of the party, a village postmaster, clothed with authority by government, may "*determine*"—ah, sir, that's the word he uses—may "DETERMINE" whether he will deliver the papers they have ordered and paid for, or not. Sir, these men, who were brought up in a free State, and learned to love liberty, will never submit to such laws, anywhere. If Southern gentlemen are content to have these petty tools of a despotism more intolerant than that of Austria, *determine* what papers they may read, they can do so; but I can vouch for a few millions at the North who will take what papers they please, and who would not give up the right to read what they liked, and say what they pleased, for a home in the finest country in the world.

This freedom of speech and of the press have cost too much blood and suffering in the past, to be given up now for the sake of accommodating a few thousands of an aristocracy, who rob one class of *all* their rights, and then bid their poorer neighbors relinquish *half* of theirs, so they may live on in security. But go from the post office to the church, and the trouble increases. There are some men who want one of the Beecher family to preach to *them;* but this will not answer, and what shall they do? Gentlemen may say that it is not necessary to my happiness that I should hear Beecher preach, or read the New York Tribune. I reply that I am the best judge of that; and I wish to say distinctly, that I will read such papers as I please, and hear such preaching as I prefer, when out of Washington, without leave asked of government or the Democratic party; and that I never will consent to the enactment of any laws in United States Territories by which the people are robbed of these precious rights and privileges.

But here a specious plea is put in, and we are told to bear with this awhile till the population is large enough for a State, as it will be very soon, and then let the majority decide whether it shall be a slave State or not; and if it be a slave State, acquiesce, or move away, and let the majority govern. Sir, I would like to know what opportunity the friends of freedom have under the laws to be heard. We remember the laws enacted in Kansas, and which government was obliged to repeal, so indignant were a vast number of the people of the North on account of them. But think you Southern men will not call for such laws again? Sir, they are demanding them now. On the 23d day of February last, a distinguished Southern Senator introduced a bill entitled "An act to punish offences against slave property in the Territory of Kansas." The 12th section of this bill reads as follows: "*If any free person by speaking or writing assert or maintain that persons have not the right to hold slaves in the Territory of Kansas*, or shall introduce into the said Territory, print, publish, write, circulate, or cause to be introduced into the said Territory, written, printed, published, or circulated in said Territory, any book, paper, magazine, pamphlet, or circular containing any denial of the right of persons to hold slaves in said Territory, *such persons shall be deemed guilty of felony, and punished by imprisonment at hard labor for a term not less than two years nor more than five years.*" What a beautiful law! What despot in the dark ages punished freedom of speech with more severity? Yet this is a Republic, and these are Democrats who ask for such laws in the middle of the nineteenth century, and who ask for a new lease of power from the people, that they may enact such laws in every Territory of the United States.

And here in the face of these enactments you say the people, when they meet to frame a constitution before they become a State, may DECIDE whether they will have slavery or not in their constitution. What an insult is this! How are the friends of freedom to do anything? They can't hold a public meeting; they can't take a paper, or circulate a tract that denounces slavery; they can't tell their neighbor slavery is wrong and ought to be prohibited in their constitution. No, these are all offences against the law, and punished by confinement in the penitentiary. Should they detect one circulating the Helper book, they might think imprisonment too mild a punishment for him, and swing him off on the first tree they came to. We see how they enforce these laws in the Southern States, and similar laws will always be enacted wherever slavery is established. They call the Republican party a sectional party, because we do not have an electoral ticket in many of the Southern States. Sir, a man can not vote the Republican ticket at the South if he desires to, and a public meeting to advocate our principles cannot be held in the South anywhere except in two or three localities. How can there be a party without a press or power to hold a public meeting for the advocacy of these principles. In Delaware recently the grand jury indicted a postmaster for delivering the New York Tribune to subscribers, and this tyrannical interference with those rights every citizen ought to enjoy without molestation, is almost universal at the South. What a *thing* a man *may* become by submission to laws like these, abdicating his manhood and crawling through life not daring to speak till he knows what he may be allowed to say, nor take a paper unless some petty postmaster "determines" for him that he may read

5413

it. And this is a modern Democrat, graduating at a Southern school of politics, and aspiring to the leadership of the people.

Mr. Chairman, the South have territory enough now to support a population of one hundred millions. There they can enact such laws as they deem necessary to the security of life and property, and within those limits I think they must remain. I have no desire to molest or disturb them at all, nor shall I go there to establish a free press; but I never will consent to extend slavery over any more territory, or to the enactment of those laws that are necessary to its security; and I know that hundreds of thousands think as I do. I believe we shall succeed in checking the progress of this moral and political plague—but the advocates of slavery are greatly elated with their successes, and assail whatever stands in their way with a boldness worthy of a better cause. A distinguished Senator, in a late address on education, denounced the standard works of the world on moral science, because they all condemn slavery. But, as slavery is *certainly right*, those books are not; and he says: "Why may not some Southern writer prepare a work on moral science which shall *supersede* both Paley and Wayland?" Sure enough, why not? and so educate the whole world into a belief that slavery is morally right. But their assaults upon free-labor, and their expressions of contempt for it, are enough to rouse the indignation of all workingmen who believe that labor is an honest, honorable, and dignified way of supporting themselves, and those who are dependent on them. Yet, when men buy and sell their laborers and mechanics, they cannot be expected to have much respect for them. "Do you want to hire a carpenter?" said a young man I knew who went South, to a gentleman evidently making preparations to build. "No," said he, "I *bought one* last week." They can buy blacksmiths and carpenters as well as ordinary laborers. I cut the following advertisement from a Savannah paper lately:

"CAPERS & HEYWARD will sell at private sale five intelligent and competent BOOT AND 'SHOEMAKERS, of the most unexceptionable character. They would also make capable 'house servants. The best of references given as to capacity, honesty, and sobriety. 'Apply at our office, south side of Adger wharf."

How does this sound to Northern shoemakers? No strikes there for higher wages. Oh! no; they are taken care of when sick, and fed and clothed at a cost of about fifty dollars per annum, each; and this is a better consideration for the laborer than one of liberty, according to these Democratic statesmen. In fact, men who labor for a livelihood *are* slaves, in their estimation. A distinguished Senator (Hammond) says: "Your *whole hireling class of manual laborers* and operatives, as you call them, *are essentially slaves.*" Another eminent Senator says that slavery is the *natural condition of the laborer*; that it has existed in all ages of the world, and been the source of every great civilization; while, on the contrary, *free-labor* is an untried experiment, which may work well and may not, though *his* opinion inclines to the latter idea. Jefferson, and the statesmen of his day, *believed* that man has by nature certain *inalienable rights*. But one of the most eminent of Southern Senators, who is certainly a man of great abilities, *denies* that man has *any natural or inherent rights*; and says, *all he can attain to are purely conventional, and such as other men* may allow him. Of course, then, when one class of men have power enough to enslave others, it is all right, and the slave cannot plead that he is wronged at all. The condition of free white labor in the slave States is such as to influence the minds of men in favor of the idea that all laborers would be in a better condition if they were slaves. At least, Southern men, resolved to defend slavery, may naturally come to this conclusion from what they see around them. We have some high colored descriptions of the happy condition of the free white laborers at the South, from gentlemen on this floor. It would not become me to dispute the correctness of these statements with regard to those localities where they reside, and of which they speak especially. But we have well authenticated accounts of the condition of the free white laborers at the South, which are of a different character entirely. Most of them agree that the non-slaveholder is a staunch defender of the peculiar institution; but this is not surprising when we reflect on *their* belief that the abolition of slavery would elevate the negro to an equality with themselves, and destroy that *caste*, which is the source of their pride and independence of feeling. In the lowest depth of wretchedness to which he can descend, the poor white man feels that there is a lower deep still, and a class over whom he can tyrannize, and for whom he can still feel contempt.

5.44

But I wish to present some facts showing the effect of slavery on free laborers in the slave States. And first: education is grossly neglected, and ignorance prevails to an alarming extent. According to the census of 1850, there were 508,000 adult whites in the slave States who could not read and write. The number in the free States at the same time, was about 100,000 less, though the white population was twice as large. And there is another fact in connection with this: the larger number of these persons in the free States belong to the foreign born population; while in the South, the majority are natives of the States where they reside. Poverty and degradation are the fruits of this excessive ignorance; and I quote from men well acquainted with these free whites and their condition in society.

Gov. Hammond, in an address before the South Carolina Institute, in 1850, speaking of the poor whites, says:

"They obtain a precarious subsistence by occasional jobs, by hunting, by fishing, by 'plundering fields or folds, and too often by what is in its effects far worse—trading with 'slaves, and seducing them to plunder for their benefit."

A writer in De Bow's Review, which I presume is good authority, in an article advocating the introduction of manufactures at the South for the purpose of employing the poor white population, and rescuing them from the present degraded condition, in alluding to the partial success of an experiment in a small village, says:

"My experience at Graniteville has satisfied me, that unless our poor people can be 'brought together in villages, and some means of employment afforded them, it will be an 'utterly hopeless effort to undertake to educate them. * * * * We have 'collected at that place about eight hundred people, and as likely looking a set of country 'girls as may be found—industrious and orderly people, but deplorably ignorant, three-'fourths of the adults not being able to read, or to write their names. * * * 'With the aid of ministers of the Gospel on the spot, to preach to them and lecture them 'on the subject, we have obtained but about sixty children for our school, of about a 'hundred which are in this place. We are satisfied that nothing but time and patience 'will enable us to bring them all out." * * * * * * * * *

And again, from the same article, I give the following extract:

"While we are aware that the Northern and Eastern States find no difficulty in edu-'cating their poor, we are ready to despair of success in the matter, for even penal laws 'against the neglect of education would fail to bring many of our country people to send 'their children to school. * * * I have long been under the impression, and 'every day's experience has strengthened my convictions, that the evils exist in 'the wholly neglected condition of this class of persons. Any man who is an observer 'of things could hardly pass through our country without being struck with the fact 'that all the capital, enterprise, and intelligence, is employed in directing slave labor; 'and the consequence is, that a large portion of our poor white people are wholly ne-'glected, and are suffered to while away an existence in a state but one step in advance 'of the Indian of the forest. It is an evil of vast magnitude, and nothing but a change 'in public sentiment will effect its cure. These people must be brought into daily con-'tact with the rich and intelligent—they must be stimulated to mental action, and taught 'to appreciate education and the comforts of civilized life."

I beg leave to differ with the writer, and affirm that no change in public sentiment can reach this evil. Nothing but a change of institutions will prove effectual. Another extract alludes to the influence of slavery in degrading labor:

"It is not to be disguised, nor can it be successfully controverted, that a degree and 'extent of poverty and destitution exist in the Southern States, among a certain class of 'people, almost unknown in the manufacturing districts of the North. The poor white 'man will endure the evils of pinching poverty, rather than engage in servile labor under 'the existing state of things, even were employment afforded him, which is not general. 'The white female is not wanted at service, and if she were, she would, however hum-'ble in the scale of society, consider such service a degree of degradation to which she 'could not condescend; and she has, therefore, no resource but to suffer the pangs of 'want and wretchedness. Boys and girls, by thousands, destitute both of employment 'and the means of education, grow up to ignorance and poverty, and, too many of them, 'vice and crime."

This condition of things might be expected in a State where the most of the mechanics and laborers were mere chattels, and sold in market like cattle and horses. Labor must necessarily be degrading there. There are some employments white men may engage in, but what they term *menial services* must be performed by slaves. An eloquent Senator, in a late speech, says: "I should like to see one of the gentlemen on the other [Republican] side try to get a white man to black his boots or curry his horse, in Texas—he might get curried himself!"

Mr. Chairman, I am perfectly willing the people in Texas should do as they please about this or that kind of work, and that their Representatives should say what they please about labor, and term some kinds of service menial and degrading, if they think so. There is nothing new about it; I have heard this kind of talk for many years. It does not sound much like "the grand utterance of the early gods,"—Franklin, Sherman, and their associates, who lived in those days when there were giants in the land. It *may* do for Southern latitudes, but I pray God in his mercy to preserve the young men of the North from a belief in it.

I was born in the mountains of New England, and brought up, thank God, to work, and to believe in the dignity of labor, and that it was necessary to the health and happiness of the man, and to the progress and improvement of the human race. I was not taught that any man could be degraded by the faithful performance of any needed service; and to-day I had rather earn my bread by any honest employment, however humble, than by raising slaves for market. If any labor that is necessary is degrading to freemen, then slavery should be universal, and I protest against the premises and the conclusion.

It is but a short time since all laborers were slaves; and despite the opinions of Democratic statesmen, I see nothing in the history of those days that tempts me to desire a return of them, if it were possible. The useful arts were almost unknown. There were men of genius—sculptors who could almost make the marble breathe, architects who built churches, and cathedrals, and palaces, of marvelous beauty, at the bidding of kings—but they couldn't make a plough, or build a saw-mill. Labor-saving machinery was unknown; and not until the laborer was FREE and educated did the arts make any progress, and the world begin to move. But with the intelligent workman came the invention of machinery for lightening toil, and *then* two hands became ten thousand, and the world was filled with wonders. The South were commencing the cultivation of cotton, but separating the seed was a slow and expensive process, and placed a limit to its production. One of that despised class among Southern men, who can not live there now, a Yankee schoolmaster, invented the cotton-gin, by which an immense amount of labor was saved, and countless millions added to the wealth of the cotton-growing States. Richard Arkwright, who was engaged in the *menial* occupation of a barber, invented machinery for spinning; the power-loom soon followed, and cotton was king.

In every department of industry we have witnessed the same miraculous transformations and the same wonderful progress, till we cease to be astonished, and these miracles in the world of mechanics excite no surprise. But what creations of wealth and power and splendor have we witnessed! An English statesman, not long ago, declared that if it were necessary for England to go to war, she could, by a trifling addition to the income tax, which would not be felt in such an emergency, raise one hundred millions of dollars to carry it on—not for a year or two, but ten of them, if necessary. How is it, that thirty millions of people have become so rich and powerful? Her troops and her fleets are all over the world. She can furnish the monarchs of Europe with money, and hire their armies if needed, to fight her battles. From whence comes this ever-increasing wealth—this power to control the world?

Mr. Chairman, it is the product of *intelligent labor*, that can multiply power to any extent to accomplish its purposes, and sometimes enables one man to perform the labor of a thousand. It is said the machinery in operation in England can do as much work as *four hundred million of men.* Therein you find the secret of her wealth and power: four hundred million of *producers*, and only thirty million of consumers. Is her wealth a wonder now? What they *have* done in England, we are doing in the free States now. We have created the steam engine, to toil for us, and compelled the lightning to carry our thoughts. The laborer is hundred-handed now, and the *elements* are *his* slaves. If we do not live as long as Methusaleh, we can do as much in eighty years as he could in eight hundred. We have perfected that marvel of mechanism, the printing press, that we may educate the toiling millions, and make ignorance and slavery alike impossible.

This multiplication of power, and consequent increase of wealth, by the creation of machinery—this education and elevation of the masses, with the introduction of the comforts and luxuries of life to the home of the humblest workmen—is the effect of *free labor.* I say FREE LABOR, because it was *first free*, and *then intelligent* and *creative*, filling the world with the trophies of its triumphs, and illuminating the history of our times with the glory of its achievements.

I trust our youth, as they advance to manhood, will learn to love labor, and comprehend its dignity and importance. Let them not be surprised if some speak of it with contempt, for the world is but just emerging from forty centuries of serfdom and slavery, and but a small portion of the masses have compelled an acknowledgment of their rights, and obtained that education so necessary to their happiness and success in life. But these prejudices will pass away, as education becomes universal; for intelligence will lend dignity to every calling and pursuit. Nothing that *needs* to be done can degrade him who does it, if it is *well* done. *No matter what the employment,* "THE MAN'S THE MAN FOR ALL THAT."

Thirty years ago, there was a day laborer splitting rails on a farm in Illinois, and on the 4th of March next, if God spares his life, HE WILL BE PRESIDENT of the United States. Let our young men read *his* life, and follow his example, imitate his industry, his integrity, and they will be respected and not go down to the grave unheard of and unknown. What a comment on our free institutions is the career of Abraham Lincoln. I wish to say a few words in reply to the arguments I hear in defense of slavery. I regret the necessity for it. Slavery is a legacy of the past to the present, and the problem of its perpetuity or its abolition is not easily solved. The national government has nothing to do with slavery in the States, and do not propose to meddle with it. But we have Territories, and let us agree that they shall remain free till they become States; after that, if they choose to establish slavery nobody can prevent them. Slavery in the States needs no outlet at present. There is room enough for a score of years to come for all the slaves you own where you have a fine climate and fertile soil. Let us agree to this, and put an end to this everlasting discussion of abstract principles, and attend to the business and interests of the people. Why not? There is but one difficulty in the way—free speech and a free press. You think we should stop the discussion of the question of slavery at the North. The eminent Senator from Illinois, if I understand him, proposes to enact a law by which he says he can repress the "irrepressible conflict" among us, that is break up anti-slavery societies, and put down anti-slavery papers and public meetings. Was there ever madness like this? Do gentlemen suppose we could do this if we would, or would do it if we could? The armies of Napoleon are not sufficient for such an undertaking. If our men assail slavery, yours must answer them, and if you get worsted we shall think you are on the wrong side. If your institutions can't stand these discussions, what will you do about it? Suppose you secede, that will do no good unless you could cut your Territory loose from ours and sail off to Asia. No; we are all here together, and there is no help for it. You may as well take this question out of Congress, and if you don't wish to answer our Northern speakers and presses who assail you, you can keep still. I presume we shall make noise enough for both sides. But you say you won't submit to this; you are too rich and powerful. The world must have cotton and can't get it unless you grow it and sell it; and unless we behave better, you will stop trading with us, ruin the business of New York and bring the whole North to their knees again. Well they have been in the habit of kneeling so long, I don't know but they would, but I guess *not now.* This great idea of the wealth and power of the South somehow revives my recollection of the arrogance of the Assyrian monarch, who standing among his princes like a planter among his slaves, exclaimed: "*Is not this great Babylon which I have builded.*" Like him you may see power suddenly pass away like the dreams of morning and the early dew. But I must say a word about this cotton argument in defence of slavery. You say the world must have cotton, and that the loss of a single crop would be an awful calamity to England. *What would it be to the South!* I fancy Old and New England both could live as long without cotton as you could without the pay for it. You say too we can't raise cotton with free labor, slaves are indispensable to its cultivation, and so slavery must be eternal if cotton is. This may be so. I don't believe it. Free labor has never been fairly tried in the cultivation of cotton, but the immense and increasing profits of this business will tempt men sooner or later to try it. I don't know how they will succeed now, but I do know free labor has always accomplished what it has undertaken. He is a bold man, not a wise one, who affirms anything is impossible *except* to perpetuate slavery. Another argument for slavery is based on the inferiority of the race. If good for anything it applies to all inferior races, white or black, but it is not worth a moment's notice.

It is the old argument kings and princes use in defence of despotism, and will not do for this meridian.

If a man is a vagrant, or begger, or a criminal, let the law say what shall be done with him; but inferiority of intellect confers no right on any State, or person, to enslaves another. Other reasons are urged in its favor, but they need no reply. The *damning fact* that the institution of slavery *will not bear examination*, is sufficient answer to all of them. Wherever it exists, *freedom of speech*, is necessarily unknown. The penalty of speaking against it is death or banishment. The PRESS and the PULPIT must be muzzled ere slavery feels secure.

In these reasons against the extension of slavery, we have not considered the condition of the slaver, but the effect of it on the free white men of the country, and that condemns it everywhere.

In New Mexico, slavery is not only established and protected by the severest laws, but free white men, who hire by the year, have no legal protection against ill treatment. The courts are forbidden to take cognizance of their complants against their employers, for any violence done them. And thus wherever this institution is established in a new Territory, every night we have been wont to regard as sacred, is trampled under foot—and not slaves alone, but free men must suffer. The slaveholder is as supreme as the Sultan of Turkey, and allows less of liberty than the Mahomedan despot. The prevalent customs are unlike those of highly civilized States. Pistols and other weapoes are pocket companions, and men go armed in this way for the same reason that kings keep up standing armies for fear of insurrection.

This readiness to resort to force at any moment, is attended with frightful results. Street fights are not unusual, and friends and neighbors are shot down in a moment of excitement, for a fancied insult. The "laws of honor" are substituted for the law of the land and the law of God, and the duellist often finds his calling a round in the ladder of preferment. Of course there are thousands of excellent persons in all such communities who are better than their laws and institutions, but I speak of the controlling portion of society, and of the manner in which their customs and usages appear to others. I have no desire to say harsh things of slavery or slaveholders, though I have been compelled to listen to the fiercest denunciations of the free States and free men since this session commenced. Let the slave States retain and *enjoy* their *peculiar* institution as long as they please, but do not ask us to consecrate one foot more of Territory *now free*, to the "*everlasting curse of human bondage.*"

I have read a recent speech by a member of this House, who resides on the borders ot the slave States, and he seems to think the Borderers know more about slavery than we do further North. Perhaps so; but I remember an old Scotch proverb, that "*The border is always the worst part of the ueb,*" and *that* may be true. I don't know. He makes a long speech to prove the Republican party are in favor of the social equality of the negro. No reply to this is needed at the North. It was not made for our section of the country, but for *Southern* consumption, and an immense edition of it has been sent off that way, with a view to strengthen the prejudices of the people against the Republican party. I have no desire to follow him through the filthy details of the evidence he brings forward to fortify his assertions, but I doubt if any jury would find a man guilty of stealing five dollars on such evidence as that. He gives an account of a ball held at Five Points in the city of New York, where white women and negroes mingled "in sweet confusion in the mazy dance." I believe that is the strongest Democratic ward in the city, and I doubt if a Republican vote was ever polled there. The Democratic *majority* in that city is larger than the entire vote of some Southern *States;* and I believe some papers printed there—not Republican—say it is the worst-governed city in the civilized world. Probably the party have managed it much as they have the national government. There, too, Five Points and Fifth Avenue unite in voting the Democratic ticket—the one by instinct, the other for Southern trade and the spoils of office. This may explain why they suffer such scandalous affairs to take place in the commercial capital of our country; but what the Republican party have to do with it, passeth my comprehension.

Then, he has a story taken from some paper about a beautiful white girl eloping and marrying a negro in Michigan. He probably thought it *might* be true, but there is not a particle of any foundation for it. Andrew Robinson, Esq., writes to the Detroit Advertiser, from the town where the scene is laid, and says he is assessor of the town, and has been for six years, and knows every person in it; that no such persons ever lived there, and nothing of the kind has taken place there, or anywhere in the vicinity. I presume the most of the stories he has published are as destitute of truth as this is. Such a case may occur once in a long time, or among millions of people, but I venture the assertion, that where one white woman marries a negro in a Republicaa State, a hundred white men can be found in Democratic States, who sell *their own children* because they are tainted with African blood. An eminent Southern statesman, many years since, said, in substance, that the African race was bleaching out rapidly at the South, and the returns of the census confirm the statement. There are hundreds of thousands of mulattos, quadroons and octoroons—men and women bleached and partially bleached—and the number is rapidly increasing; and the whole African race at the South are growing whiter and whiter every day. As there are no Republicans in these States, this must be considered Democratic, and of course all right.

But my time is expiring, and I must close.

The Democracy have been in power for eight years past, and did as they pleased in all respects; and what is the result? I cannot speak of the waste of the public treasure in detail, but merely state the fact that while the party could not spare $50,000 for improving the St. Clair Flats, they have managed to expend over *one hundred millions of dollars* more in the eight years than our governnment did the first forty years of its existence, which included the entire expense of the last war with England. They draw a doleful picture of the present condition of the country, and I presume they tell the truth. They found it peaceful and prosperous, no dissensions, and no public debt, and they have saddled us with a national debt of some magnitude, created a great sectional party, and filled the whole country with strife, and lashed the popular feeling into fury. The people are weary of this useless agitation and of the policy of the party that compel its adoption, and have given them notice to quit the capital on the 4th of March next. They have nominated an HONEST MAN for the presidency, and they will elect him. He will take possession on the 4th of March, and say to this troubled sea of politics: "*Be still!*"—*and there will be a great calm.*

We have been told the South will not suffer us to inaugurate a Republican President; that they will blow us out of the capital at the cannon's mouth, secede from the North, and all that. Well, I have sometimes, when riding on a train of cars, seen a little dog rush out of a farm-house, yelping furiously at the locomotive, as if he expected to drive it off the track. But the iron horse ran the fastest, and the worst of all was, that every time the poor dog opened his mouth to bark, *he lost ground.* He could not bark and run too. It is so with those who are denouncing the Republican party, and preaching disunion. Every time they open their mouths, they lose ground.

Mr. Chairman, I think they will conclude to let us inaugurate Lincoln; that is my opinion. But seriously, this talk about disunion is all folly, and every sane man knows it. So long as the President administers the government in accordance with the law and the constitution, he will be obeyed; but should he attempt to violate either, the people everywhere would consign him to a traitor's doom. Disunion is impossible. We bought the Southwest because we would not permit a foreign power to hold possession of the mouth of the Mississippi. We paid for it, and we shall keep it—that you can depend on. Mr. Chairman, we have been advised to buy Cuba, at a cost of three hundred millions of dollars, and admit her into the Union. Well, suppose we should. If secession be constitutional, the first time we refused to do what her members in Congress demand, Cuba would secede and leave us—minus the "Gem of the Antilles" and three hundred millions of dollars. I think our Democratic brothers would object to that. Sir, disunion is impossible, and no Northern armies will be found necessary to prevent it. There are hundreds of thousands of Southern patriots, who will never see this Union sundered—never, *never*, NEVER! Read the electric words that came leaping from the heart of that glorious old man —Robert J. Breckenridge, of Kentucky—rebuking these disunion doctrines. He tells us that he loves the South, and loves her institutions; but, said he, "*I am an* AMERICAN CITIZEN, *and I deny, with uplifted hand, the right of any Court, any Congress, any President, any State, or any combination of States under heaven, to abolish from among man* THAT HIGHEST OF ALL HUMAN TITLES." Paint these words on your banners, and hundreds of thousands of Southern hearts would beat like a drum in battle at the sight of them. They love this Union, and they will preserve it, and bequeath it to their posterity in all its vastness, stretching from the Atlantic to the Pacific, and from the Great Lakes to the Gulf of Mexico, united, as of old, and more glorious than ever. And when Death shall find them under the more than Italian splendor of their sunny skies, the Flag of their Country will be floating in every sea and every clime; its starry beauty undimmed, and the great nation, of whose power it is the symbol, still united, and feared and honored throughout the world!

www.ingramcontent.com/pod-product-compliance
Lightning Source LLC
LaVergne TN
LVHW020643110826
845149LV00004B/1337
* 9 7 8 1 4 1 8 1 9 0 0 9 5 *